Written and compiled by Sophie Piper
This edition copyright © 2014 Lion Hudson

The right of the illustrators listed on p. 46 to be identified as the illustrators of this work has been asserted them in accordance with the Copyright, Designs and Patents Act 1988.

Published by Lion Children's Books
an imprint of
Lion Hudson plc
Wilkinson House, Jordan Hill Road,
Oxford OX2 8DR, England
www.lionhudson.com/lionchildrens
ISBN 978 0 7459 6503 1

First edition 2009
This edition 2014

A catalogue record for this book is available from the British Library

Printed and bound in China, November 2013, LH06

THE LION BOOK OF

POEMS &
PRAYERS
for Easter

LION
CHILDREN'S

Contents

Dreams

Hold fast to dreams
For if dreams die
Life is a broken-winged bird
That cannot fly.

Hold fast to dreams
For when dreams go
Life is a barren field
Frozen with snow.

Langston Hughes
(1902–1967)

Thaw

Over the land freckled with snow half-thawed
The speculating rooks at their nests cawed
And saw from elm-tops, delicate as flower of grass,
What we below could not see, Winter pass.

Edward Thomas (1878–1917)

9

There is a green hill

There is a green hill far away,
Without a city wall,
Where the dear Lord was crucified
Who died to save us all.

We may not know, we cannot tell,
What pains he had to bear,
But we believe it was for us
He hung and suffered there.

He died that we might be forgiven,
He died to make us good;
That we might go at last to heaven,
Saved by his Precious Blood.

10

There was no other good enough
To pay the price of sin;
He only could unlock the gate
Of heaven, and let us in.

O, dearly, dearly has he loved,
And we must love him too,
And trust in his redeeming Blood,
And try his works to do.

Mrs C.F. Alexander (1818–95)

Were you there?

Were you there when they crucified my Lord?
Were you there when they crucified my Lord?
Oh! sometimes it causes me to tremble, tremble,
   tremble.
Were you there when they crucified my Lord?

Were you there when they nailed him to the tree?
Were you there when they nailed him to the tree?
Oh! sometimes it causes me to tremble, tremble,
  tremble.
Were you there when they nailed him to the tree?

Were you there when they laid him in the tomb?
Were you there when they laid him in the tomb?
Oh! sometimes it causes me to tremble, tremble,
  tremble.
Were you there when they laid him in the tomb?

Were you there when he rose up from the dead?
Were you there when he rose up from the dead?
Oh! sometimes I feel like shouting, 'Glory!
  Hallelujah!'
Were you there when he rose up from the dead?

African-American spiritual

The Easter garden

In the Easter garden
the leaves are turning green;
in the Easter garden
the risen Lord is seen.

In the Easter garden
we know that God above
brings us all to heaven
through Jesus and his love.

Resurrection

The autumn leaves were laid to rest
But now the trees are green,
And signs that God brings all to life
Throughout the world are seen.

And Jesus is alive, they say,
And death is not the end.
We rise again in heaven's light
With Jesus as our friend.

All things right

The winter branches were bare and grey
But now the blossom is white,
And Christ was hung on a tree to die
But God has put all things right.

The tree of thorns

The tree of thorns
is dressed in white
for resurrection day;
and joy springs from
the underworld
now death is put away.

17

New life

Let me capture springtime
Bright with yellow flowers
Twittering with birdsong
Glittering with showers.

Let me capture summer
Blue with sea and sky
Lazy like the seabirds
Drifting in the sky.

Let me capture autumn's
Cloak of red and gold
Darned with threads of silver
As the year grows old.

Set me free from winter's
Prison bars of rain
From earth's dark decaying
Let life spring again.

Life comes leaping

Winter death
and springtime breath;
winter grief
and springtime leaf;
winter sleep
but life comes leaping
from the darkest deep.

The Lamb

Little Lamb, who made thee?
Does thou know who made thee?
Gave thee life, and bid thee feed,
By the stream and o'er the mead;
Gave thee clothing of delight,
Softest clothing, woolly, bright;
Gave thee such a tender voice,
Making all the vales rejoice?
Little Lamb, who made thee?
Does thou know who made thee?

Little Lamb, I'll tell thee,
Little Lamb, I'll tell thee:
He is called by thy name
For he calls himself the Lamb:
He is meek, and he is mild;
He became a little child.
I a child, and thou a lamb,
We are called by his name,
Little Lamb, God bless thee!
Little Lamb, God bless thee!

William Blake (1757–1827)

Spring

Sun waker
Music maker
Bud popper
Bird hopper
Crocus grower
Shoot shower
Daffodil dabbler
Brook babbler
Breeze puffer
Petal fluffer
Duckweed floater
Blossom bloater
Cuckoo spotter
Flowerbed plotter
Leaf sprouter

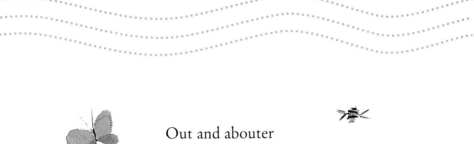

Out and abouter
Stream rusher
Waterfall gusher
Lamb lifter
Cloud drifter
Squirrel tumbler
Bee bumbler
Butterfly singer
New life bringer.

Coral Rumble

23

To make a prairie

To make a prairie it takes a clover
   and one bee,
One clover, and a bee.
And revery.
The revery alone will do,
If bees are few.

Emily Dickinson (1830–1886)

Merrily, merrily

Merrily, merrily,
All the spring,
Merrily, merrily
Small birds sing.
All through April,
All through May,
Small birds merrily
Carol all day.

Rodney Bennett

25

Conspiracy

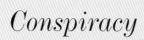

Beware! Be on your guard!
Spring has hatched a plot.

The grass has formed an underground
  movement
and the seeds are ready to shoot on sight.

The speckled pond spawn may quiver
  now but soon the frogs will be
  marching.

Deep within their woollen cocoons
  the grubs are earning their wings,
  getting ready to take control of the
  skies.

Beware! Be on your guard!
Spring is ready to drive winter from the
  land.

Snowdrop

The snowdrop heard that spring had come
and rushed out to the light –
then bent her head, ashamed to show
her underwear of white.

I wandered lonely as a cloud

I wandered lonely as a cloud
That floats on high o'er vales and hills,
When all at once I saw a crowd,
A host, of golden daffodils;
Beside the lake, beneath the trees,
Fluttering and dancing in the breeze.

Continuous as the stars that shine
And twinkle on the milky way,
They stretched in never-ending line
Along the margin of a bay:
Ten thousand saw I at a glance,
Tossing their heads in sprightly dance.

The waves beside them danced; but they
Out-did the sparkling leaves in glee:
A poet could not be but gay,
In such a jocund company:
I gazed – and gazed – but little thought
What wealth the show to me had brought:

For oft, when on my couch I lie
In vacant or in pensive mood,
They flash upon that inward eye
Which is the bliss of solitude;
And then my heart with pleasure fills,
And dances with the daffodils.

William Wordsworth (1770–1850)

Easter egg hunt

As you search for Easter eggs
I hope that you will find
the signs that spring has come
and left the winter far behind.

As you eat your Easter eggs
I hope that you will hear
the real birds are singing out
to welcome in the year.

When your Easter eggs are gone
I hope that you will see
the real birds have hatched their eggs
so high up in the tree.

Egg dance

Dancing in among the eggs
cannot be recommended
for if you once mistake your step
your slip cannot be mended.

The Easter bunny

The Easter bunny lives in an egg
Feasting on chocolate cream
His friends all say he's a basket case
Lost in a daffodil dream.

Rabbit habits

If Easter bunnies
lay chocolate eggs
there soon won't be
any rabbits.

They should think
of the environment
and resume
their usual habits.

Prayer of the rabbit

Thank you for the food I eat –
salad leaves so fresh and sweet,
food that keeps me fit to run
and run and run and run and run.

The truffle pig

I bought a pig for Easter
with a sniffly snoffly snuffle,
for sniffly snoffly snuffly snouts
are best for finding truffles.

At Whitsuntide I left my pig
to sleep in fields of clover,
for he had grown so corpulent
his truffling days were over.

A duck for a friend

I wish I could have a duck for a friend –
I've been thinking that now for a while,
For a duck has a beak that curls up at the ends
And it looks, to me, much like a smile.

I wish I could have a duck for a friend –
I've been thinking that all through the day,
For a duck always talks with a comforting quack
Even when you have nothing to say.

I wish I could have a duck for a friend –
I've been thinking that over again,
For a duck can be trusted to waddle close by
When you're out for a walk in the rain.

Little things

Create a space for little things:
Bejewelled bugs with buzzing wings
And pudgy grubs that bravely cling
To slender stems that bend and swing.

Create a calm for quiet things:
For timid birds too shy to sing
And breaths of wind that softly linger
In the blossom trees of spring.

Christina Goodings

Butterfly

Nothing but a butterfly
Can flutter all the day
Where the slender grasses dip
And flowers gently sway
Or tiptoe on the thistledown
Or dance upon the air
Leaving just a ripple
In the golden everywhere.

Save me a stream

Save me a clean stream, flowing
to unpolluted seas;

lend me the bare earth, growing
untamed flowers and trees.

May I share safe skies
when I wake, every day,

with birds and butterflies?
Grant me a space where I can play

with water, rocks, trees, and sand;
lend me forests, rivers, hills, and sea.

Keep me a place in this old land,
somewhere to grow, somewhere to be.

Jane Whittle

Joy

May the world turn round about,
may all things turn to right;
may the sunset thank the dawn,
the noontime bless the night;

May the rivers thank the rain,
the stormclouds bless the sea;
may the good soil thank the
    leaves,
the sunshine bless the tree;

May the rich thank those
    in need,
the children bless the old;
may the strong thank those
    who fail,
the timid bless the bold;

May the angels sing on earth,
may heaven hear our prayer;
may forgiveness, joy and peace
and love fill everywhere.

Morning has broken

Morning has broken like the first morning,
Blackbird has spoken like the first bird.
Praise for the singing! Praise for the
  morning!
Praise for them, springing from the first
  Word.

Sweet the rain's new fall sunlit from heaven,
Like the first dewfall in the first hour.
Praise for the sweetness of the wet garden,
Sprung in completeness from the first
  shower.

Mine is the sunlight! Mine is the morning
Born of the one light Eden saw play.
Praise with elation, praise every morning
Spring's recreation of the First Day!

Eleanor Farjeon (1881–1965)

45

Acknowledgments

Every effort has been made to trace and contact copyright owners. We apologize for any inadvertent omissions or errors.

Poems and prayers

pp. 14, 15, 16, 17, 18, 19, 32, 39, 42 by Lois Rock; pp. 26, 27, 30, 31, 33, 34, 35, 37 by Sophie Piper; p38 by Christina Goodings. Copyright © Lion Hudson.

p.8 'Dreams', from *The Collected Poems of Langston Hughes* by Langston Hughes, edited by Arnold Rampersad with David Roessel, Associate Editor, copyright © 1994 by The Estate of Langston Hughes. Used by permission of Alfred A. Knopf, a division of Random House, Inc and by David Higham Associates Ltd.

p.22 'Spring' by Coral Rumble taken from *My Teacher's As Wild As a Bison*, Lion Children's Books (2005). Copyright © Coral Rumble. Used with permission of the author.

p.44 'Morning has broken' by Eleanor Farjeon, taken from *The Children's Bells* by Eleanor Farjeon, OUP. Used with permission of David Higham Associates Ltd.

Illustrations

pp. 4, 6, 20–21 copyright © Christina Balit.

pp. 5, 6, 10–11, 24–25, 41, 47, the cover and endpapers copyright © Sheila Moxley.

pp. 6, 7, 8–9, 16–17, 44–45 copyright © Angelo Ruta.

pp. 6, 18–19 copyright © Elena Gomez.

pp. 7, 28–29 copyright © Alex Ayliffe.

pp. 7, 36–37 copyright © Caroline Jayne Church.

pp. 7, 38–39 copyright © Christopher Corr.

pp. 12–13 copyright © Alison Wisenfeld.

pp. 14–15 copyright © Sarah Young.

pp. 22–23 copyright © Meilo So.

pp. 26–27 copyright © Amanda Hall.

p. 31 copyright © Mique Moriuchi.

pp. 32–33 copyright © Gaby Hansen.

pp. 34–35 copyright © Tina Macnaughton.

pp. 42–43 copyright © Elena Temporin.